Gary Soto

The Library of Author Biographies™

GARY SOTO

Tamra Orr

The Rosen Publishing Group, Inc., New York

Published in 2005 by The Rosen Publishing Group, Inc.
29 East 21st Street, New York, NY 10010

Copyright © 2005 by The Rosen Publishing Group, Inc.

First Edition

All rights reserved. No part of this book may be reproduced in any form without permission in writing from the publisher, except by a reviewer.

Library of Congress Cataloging-in-Publication Data

Orr, Tamra.
  Gary Soto / Tamra Orr.— 1st ed.
     p. cm. — (The library of author biographies)
  Includes bibliographical references and index.
  ISBN 1-4042-0327-3 (library binding)
  1. Soto, Gary. 2. Authors, American—20th century—Biography. 3. Mexican American authors—Biography.
  I. Title. II. Series.
  PS3569.O72Z83 2005
  811'.54—dc22
                                                                              2004011755

Manufactured in the United States of America

Excerpt from "Gary Soto" – Video, used with permission from the Lannan Foundation, www.lannan.org.
From *Macmillan Profiles: Latino Americans*, by, Macmillan Library Reference, ©1999, Macmillan Library Reference. Reprinted by permission of The Gale Group.
"Frequently Asked Questions" from The Official Gary Soto Website (www.garysoto.com), retrieved May 2004. Used by permission of Gary Soto.
"Drought," ©1978 by Gary Soto. Used by permission of Gary Soto.
"One Last Time," from *Living Up the Street*, ©1985 by Gary Soto, Dell Publishing 1992. Used by permission of Gary Soto.
"Papi's Menudo" from *Canto Familiar*, copyright ©1995 by Gary Soto, reprinted by permission of Harcourt, Inc.
Excerpt from *Buried Onions*, copyright © 1997 by Gary Soto, reprinted by permission of Harcourt, Inc.
Excerpt from *The Afterlife*, copyright © 2003 by Gary Soto, reprinted by permission of Harcourt, Inc.
From *Fearless Fernie: Hanging Out With Fernie & Me* by Gary Soto, Illustrated by Regan Dunnick, copyright © 2002 by Gary Soto, text. Used by permission of G.P. Putnam's Sons, A Division of Penguin Young Readers Group, A Member of Penguin Group (USA) Inc., 345 Hudson Street, New York, NY 10014
From *Various Gary Soto Poems* © by Gary Soto Used with permission of Chronicle Books LLC, San Francisco. Visit ChronicleBooks.com
"The Jacket" from *The Effects of Knut Hamsun on a Fresno Boy: Recollections and Short Essays* by Gary Soto. Copyright © 1983, 2001 by Gary Soto. Reprinted by permission of Persea Books, Inc. (New York)
"This Man" and "Getting It Done" from *The Effects of Knut Hamsun on a Fresno Boy: Recollections and Short Essays* by Gary Soto. Copyright © 1983, 2001 by Gary Soto. Reprinted by permission of Persea Books, Inc. (New York)
"Blue" from *The Effects of Knut Hamsun on a Fresno Boy: Recollections and Short Essays* by Gary Soto. Copyright © 1983, 2001 by Gary Soto. Reprinted by permission of Persea Books, Inc. (New York)

Table of Contents

	Introduction	7
1.	A Childhood of Hard Work	11
2.	Falling in Love with Reading and Writing	21
3.	Writing for a New Audience	28
4.	Stories for Younger Readers	41
5.	Soto's Poetry	49
6.	Seeing Soto's Stories	67
	Interview with Gary Soto	73
	Selected Reviews from *School Library Journal*	80
	Timeline	90
	List of Selected Works	92
	List of Selected Awards	96
	Glossary	98
	For More Information	100
	For Further Reading	101
	Bibliography	103
	Source Notes	106
	Index	110

Introduction

It is hard to pinpoint what one factor has made Gary Soto the popular author he is today. Is it because he is one of the first young adult writers to devote himself exclusively to detailing the Mexican American experience? Not only is he a Chicano, but everything he writes—stories, books, and poems—centers completely on Chicano characters. "I don't talk about ethnicity," he says. "I show ethnicity."[1]

All of his writing centers on his own life or the lives of fictional people embodying and expressing their Mexican heritage. Much of Soto's work is autobiographical in that he writes a lot about growing up as a

Mexican American. It is important to him to create and share new stories about his heritage. Soto says, "There are many different kinds of writers. Some people like to write things that are factual and historical. For me, the joy of being a writer is to take things I see and hear and then rearrange them. I like to tamper with reality and create new possibilities."[2] When fellow Mexican American author Alejandro Morales asked Soto during a recorded interview if it is a burden being a Chicano writer, he replied, "No. It is a privilege."[3]

Soto's work, which includes picture books for young children and novels for adults, almost always includes a glossary of Mexican words and phrases to help readers understand and learn the language that his various characters use. Although most of Soto's writing is peppered with Spanish words and expressions, his themes remain both very personal and entirely universal. This allows readers, regardless of their cultural backgrounds, to be able to relate to his stories.

One of the reasons that Soto is a respected author is that he experiments with various types of writing rather than sticking to any single form. Unlike many authors, Soto has dabbled in everything from fictional short stories to poems

Introduction

to plays. His autobiographical essays about his childhood and adult life are just as popular as his books of poetry. He writes adult fiction as entertainingly as he does children's picture books. Soto even wrote a libretto for his children's book *Nerdlandia* for the Los Angeles opera. In addition, he has produced, directed, and written three films: *The Bike*, *The Pool Party*, and *Novio Boy*.

Another reason that readers enjoy Soto's writing is the personal detail he adds to his work, reminding readers of themselves and their own life experiences. Whether he is writing about a young man dancing with a broom he pretends is a pretty girl or his own struggle to understand his father's death, Soto strikes a deep chord inside readers. Soto's writing leads readers to recall similar moments in their pasts, creating a bond between reader and author.

Soto's work is not always cheery and optimistic—sometimes it is raw, difficult, and painfully realistic. In a profile published in *Macmillan Profiles: Latino Americans*, Soto says, "I think even in sadness, there's a certain beauty and satisfaction."[4] He adds, "Even though I write a lot about life in the barrio, I am really writing about the feelings and experiences of most

American kids; having a pet, going to the park for a family cookout, running through a sprinkler on a hot day, and getting a bee sting!"[5]

In the end, readers may not know precisely why they enjoy Soto's writing, but they find it entertaining and enjoyable. According to *Macmillan Profiles*, Soto's works "evoke the small beauties of life that emerge from the background of daily struggles."[6] Indeed, Soto's stories, essays, and poems remind people of all ages what is important in life, what is to be remembered, cherished, and most of all, appreciated. His work leaves people looking at their lives a little more closely and, perhaps, gaining a clearer idea of what makes them all so special.

1 A Childhood of Hard Work

Despite a childhood devoid of books, Gary Soto grew up to be a highly praised, well-respected writer. Born to Mexican American parents on April 12, 1952, in Fresno, California, Soto grew up in a hardworking family where no one had the time to pick up a book, magazine, or newspaper. Books could not be found anywhere within the house, and Soto was never encouraged to read. Almost everyone in his family—other than his siblings—was illiterate and remains so. Although proud of Soto's work, his relatives do not read it but instead place the book jackets in frames to be displayed on the living room table.

Soto's grandparents had come to the United States from Mexico during the Great

Depression of the 1930s. They were farm laborers, working other people's fields for many long, exhausting hours for meager pay.

Working the Fields

Gary Soto's grandmother came to the United States after the Mexican Revolution (1910–1920) to settle in Fresno, where she met her husband. She worked in the fields around Fresno, picking grapes, oranges, plums, peaches, and cotton. She also worked in fruit-packaging factories, where she stood at a conveyor belt that carried raisins. Her job was to pluck out any leaves and pebbles mixed in among the raisins. For more than twenty years, she worked at a machine that boxed raisins until she retired at the age of sixty-five. During all this hard labor, she managed to raise several children. Soto's grandfather also worked in the fields, as did his children, including Soto's mother.

Like their parents, Soto's mother, Angie, and father, Manuel, worked physically demanding jobs for minimum wage. Gary's father packed boxes at the Sunmaid Raisin Company near Fresno, while his mother peeled potatoes at the Redi-Spuds factory. Gary, his older brother, Rick, and younger sister, Debra, spent much of their childhood doing all kinds of chores and jobs—from picking grapes and oranges to hoeing cotton and beets. Soto recalls this backbreaking, tedious work in his poem, "A Red Palm":

> You're in this dream of cotton plants.
> You raise a hoe, swing, and the first weeds
> Fall with a sigh. You take another step,
> Chop, and the sigh comes again.
> Until you yourself are breathing that way
> With each step, a sigh that will follow you into town.
>
> That's hours later. The sun is a red blister
> Coming up in your palm . . .
> Dust settles on your forehead, dirt
> Smiles under each fingernail.[1]

Feeling Trapped

When Soto was five, his father died in an industrial accident at work. As a child, he was somewhat bewildered and confused by the event. He does not remember feeling sad or crying. Instead, his most vivid recollection is of the sense of awkwardness he felt when relatives held his hand or patted his head to offer sympathy and consolation.

Shortly after his father's death, Gary and his family moved away from their south Fresno neighborhood. Later, in his essay "This Man," from a collection of essays and remembrances titled *The Effects of Knut Hamsun on a Fresno Boy*, he describes how his family changed after the loss of Manuel Soto:

> Something happened in our family without us being aware, a quiet between mother and children settled on us like dust. We went to school, ate, watched television that wasn't funny, and because mother never said anything, father, too, became the name we never said in our house. His grave was something we saw in photographs; his remembrance those clothes hanging in the back of the closet.[2]

For two years, Soto and his two siblings were raised by their mother and grandparents. His mother eventually remarried, however, and had two more children. Soto's stepfather was an alcoholic, exhausted by backbreaking and monotonous work at a factory, where he labored for long hours lifting heavy boxes onto a conveyor belt. The pressure of making ends meet—of making house payments and keeping his new wife and their five children clothed and fed—was often too great for him.

As he got older, Soto felt little hope that he would ever be able to rise above the type of life his parents and grandparents had. According to an interview in the literary journal *Ploughshares*, Soto felt that he would "marry Mexican poor, work Mexican hours, and in the end, die a Mexican death, broke and in despair."[3] This dismal, dreary prediction felt inevitable to him as he saw no other choice or possible rescue. Because simple survival was his family's main focus, their priorities were quite different from those of people in middle-class communities. For example, Soto recalls that simply staying out of prison was considered a great achievement.

Summers were often spent collecting aluminum cans to turn in for deposit money; picking grapes; or hoeing cotton. None of these jobs was easy or remotely fun. In the autobiographical piece "One Last Time," Soto describes the experience of hoeing. He says that he distracted himself from the boredom of the work by remembering incidents from school, creating imaginary girlfriends, or thinking of the clothes he would buy with the money he earned. Even so, by the end of the day, Soto's ankles, arms, and neck would ache from the labor, and his eyes would sting from the sun's glare and the dust kicked up in the cotton fields.

Though Soto says he often felt hopeless about his future, he did dare to occasionally dream about a better life. Interestingly, as a kid, Soto considered career goals that had nothing to do with writing. Although he considered becoming either a priest or a paleontologist—a scientist who studies fossils and dinosaur bones—he says he never considered becoming a writer. While Soto was still in junior high, he joined the Cadets program—a military club that helped him learn discipline and responsibility. He also hoped that being a member would help him get a girlfriend, especially if he wore his cadet's uniform decorated with various honor ribbons, color guard cords, and sergeant rank patches.

The cadet uniform might have scored a few extra points with the girls, but the coat his mother bought for him in sixth grade did not. When he needed a new jacket, he asked his mother for one. He pictured something leather, shiny black, and very cool. Instead, he received his "guacamole jacket," so named because of its bright shade of green. In an essay simply titled "The Jacket," he writes,

> I blame that jacket for those bad years. I blame my mother for her bad taste and her cheap ways. It was a sad time for the heart. With a friend I spent my sixth-grade year in a

tree in the alley, waiting for something good to happen to me in that jacket, which had become the ugly brother who tagged along wherever I went.[4]

As this bitter passage implies, Soto's childhood was often characterized by poverty, sadness, and a sense of waiting for something to change, for something good to happen. Soto's prospects for the future were not bright, and he knew it. He was reminded of this frequently, in one way or another. In his essay, "One Last Time," he writes,

> All through junior high and into my first year of high school there were those who said I would never do anything, be anyone. They said I'd work like a donkey and marry the first Mexican girl that came along. I was reminded so often, verbally and in the way I was treated at home, that I began to believe that chopping cotton might be a lifetime job for me. If not chopping cotton, then I might get lucky and find myself in a car wash or restaurant or junkyard. But it was clear; I'd work and work hard.[5]

Imagining Escape

Laughter, play, and good times were part of Soto's childhood, too, however. In his essay "Blue," Soto describes the joy of being ten years old and wandering free and climbing fruit trees with his friend Jackie. After climbing up into the trees' branches, they would freely and happily partake of the ripe, juicy fruit—plums, oranges, apricots, and peaches. Yet even these sweet and golden memories are shadowed by darkness.

> After eating our fill we stayed in the trees to talk. And about what? Girls we were in love with, God, family, mean brothers on bicycles, school fights that did no one any good. As we spoke we seldom looked at one another. Instead, we looked skyward where, if it was spring, an occasional cloud chugged by, sloshing a belly full of rain, and if it was summer, the blue was the color of a crayon. I remember that well. I also remember Jackie and the beatings his father gave him, his body balled up under a bed and screaming *Daddy No!* I said these things too, and almost cried. Because we confided in one another with our eyes on the sky, we felt less troubled when we finally did drop to the ground and went back to our homes where, however slowly, it would begin again.[6]

Soto needed to provide his own escape from the dark and troubling world around him. In "Animals All Around," from a collection of autobiographical pieces titled *Small Faces*, Soto shows his reliance on an active, incessant imagination, a trait that would play a vital and invaluable role in his adult life. Living in a neighborhood that was almost completely barren of animal life—except for dogs, cats, and the occasional squirrel—Soto describes how he and Jackie spent a great amount of time imagining that they lived in a place surrounded by deer, bears, and lions. Envious of television families like the Cleavers from *Leave It to Beaver* or the Douglases from *My Three Sons*, who went on picnics and vacations, Jackie and Gary climbed trees in the alleys behind their houses and pretended they were in Yellowstone National Park or the Grand Canyon. When even their imaginations failed them, they begged their parents to take them somewhere—anywhere—where they might see animals. The response was always an angry demand to get out of the house and do some yard or gardening work.

Despite Soto's fear about how his life would turn out, changes were coming that would soon lead him in an entirely unexpected direction. It would begin with the gloomy prospect of a minimum wage job and the possibility of being drafted into the nation's ongoing war in Vietnam. Education was one way for Gary Soto to avoid both fates.

2 Falling in Love with Reading and Writing

It was 1970, and young men from across the United States were being drafted into the military to fight in the Vietnam War. Gary Soto did not want to go, so like many others his age, he enrolled in college to avoid the draft.

Soto chose Fresno City College. It was close to home and, frankly, his high school record was not good enough to gain him entry into the bigger, more exclusive universities. He had graduated high school with a grade point average of 1.6 out of a possible 4.0. Soto has joked that perhaps one needs to be a D student to be a good writer. Not sure about his career goals, he initially decided to major in geography. Considering himself only semiliterate at the time, he hoped that geography would allow him to avoid writing. Instead, he imagined that he would simply look at maps, study rivers, and take multiple choice tests.

Discovering Poetry, Finding Love

One day, at the university library, Soto picked up a copy of *The New American Poetry Anthology*. He was particularly moved by a poem called "Unwanted" by Edward Field about a man who feels like a social outcast, or worse, totally invisible and unremarkable. Soto suddenly realized that he could communicate and release many of his pent-up feelings through the power of words. In less than an hour, he had fallen in love with the poems of Pablo Neruda, Allen Ginsberg, Lawrence Ferlinghetti, and other great poets. He was hooked on reading for the first time in his life. "I thought, Wow, wow, wow. I wanted to do this thing," he recalled in his interview in *Ploughshares*.[1]

Once Soto was introduced to poetry, he could not get enough. He took a class with poet and teacher Philip Levine, who became one of his biggest role models. He quickly changed his major to English literature and transferred to California State University, Fresno. There, he joined a group of young poets known as the Fresno School of Poets. In 1974, he graduated magna cum laude (the highest academic honor) with a bachelor of arts degree in English. Two years later, he obtained his master of fine arts degree in creative writing from the University of California, Irvine.

As Soto continued to focus on his writing, he found himself captivated by something else—love. One afternoon, he met a Japanese American woman named Carolyn Oda, and he was immediately smitten. The two were married in 1975, and Soto suddenly found that he had someone he loved and trusted to give him helpful feedback on his writing.

Soon, Soto ran everything he wrote by his wife to make sure she approved of it. If she liked a particular work, she would nod. Soto would decide which poems to save and publish based on the number of nods they received. "But I'd be so nervous, waiting for her reaction," Soto recalls in the *Ploughshares* interview. "I'd think, Oh, my God, maybe I'm a fraud, maybe this woman's going to call the Bureau of Consumer Fraud on me. I have to keep reminding myself that after all these books over all these years, I must be doing something right."[2]

Soto also calls on Carolyn when he revises his work. "My first reader is my wife; poor thing," he writes on his Web site. "I bother her almost daily as I beg, 'Carolyn, could you please look at this masterpiece?' Of course, it's not a masterpiece, but a way of getting her attention."[3]

The Birth of a Writer, the Birth of a Daughter

In 1976, Soto attended a writer's conference in Wisconsin. This was the first time he had been outside of California. He returned with what he described as an almost spiritual awakening to literature. Not long after the conference, he wrote and published his first book, a collection of poems called *The Elements of San Joaquin* (1977). As Soto notes in his essay "Who is Your Reader?," it now appeared as if his days of laboring in grape and cotton fields around Fresno were a thing of the past.

The following year brought another major accomplishment, this one of a more personal nature—Gary Soto became a father. The birth of his daughter, Mariko, was especially wonderful and meaningful to him. He had always felt a void in his life after losing his father when he was so young. As a result, he wanted to do everything in his power to ensure that Mariko would never lose him at an early age. Soto's fatherly pride, joy, and wonder are in full evidence in the following excerpt from his memoir, *The Effects of Knut Hamsun on a Fresno Boy*:

> . . . [S]he was born early morning July 21, 1978, born with her eyes open and seemingly astonished by her appearance, as if a magician had pulled her from a hat. . . She was healthy and ours, and quickly I agreed to a new title: father. . . [D]uring Mariko's babyhood, I felt like a flower that had just broken open, full of color and light and maybe even a wonderful scent. Sure, our daughter cried at night, fussed over cereals, filled her diapers with monstrous debris, and demanded time and our money, even the quarters and grimy dimes piled in the ashtray. Sure, we read books about raising a child and monitored her monthly progress, worried that she was unable to roll over in her third month, sit up at six months, waddle bravely from couch to coffee table at eleven months. But her arms and legs were plump as water balloons, and she was growing.[4]

In the beginning of his career, Soto wrote mainly for adults. In 1977, he won the U.S. Award of the International Poetry Forum for *The Elements of San Joaquin*. His work began to be published in prestigious literary publications, including the *Nation*, the *New Yorker, Paris Review, Ploughshares, Iowa Review*, and the *American Poetry Review*. Further poetry collections were published in the following years: *The Tale of Sunlight* (1978), *Father Is a Pillow Tied to a Broom* (1980), *Where Sparrows Work Hard* (1981), *Black Hair* (1985), *Who Will Know Us?* (1990), *Home Course in Religion* (1991), *New and Selected Poems* (1995), *Junior College* (1997), and *A Natural Man* (1999).

Soto began to write prose as well, including essays about his childhood, his current life, and the world around him. Soto liked the freedom he felt in prose writing to be loud and direct. With poetry, he felt his message needed to be more subtle and disguised, less obvious and blunt. The first two of these autobiographical prose collections were *Living Up the Street* (1985) and *Small Faces* (1986). *Living Up the Street* won the 1985 American Book Award, and over the years, Soto continued to win some of literature's most respected awards, including two National Endowment for the Arts fellowships for creative writing and a Guggenheim Fellowship.

In 1985, in addition to publishing his award-winning prose collection, Soto became the associate professor of English and Chicano studies at the University of California, Berkeley. This appointment coincided with an even more important career development. Many of Soto's growing legion of fans began to write him, saying that he would make a great children's and young adult author. Soto thought it was time to go in a new direction, so he set to work. Greatly excited by the possibility of captivating young people with his stories, he hoped to inspire them to become hungry readers and talented writers.

3 Writing for a New Audience

Once the idea of writing for children and teenagers was suggested to him, Gary Soto quickly and industriously began to write a wealth of poems, essays, remembrances, short stories, and novels for his new and younger readership. In some ways, it was no surprise that Soto would make a great children's author or that he would find it so easy to communicate with younger readers. Many of his adult pieces had concerned his childhood, family, and coming of age as a Mexican American in the barrios of California. All of these themes transferred extremely well to a younger audience currently living the life Soto looked back on with affection and sadness.

Gaining Momentum

In 1990, Soto issued *A Fire in My Hands*, a collection of poems, and *Baseball in April and Other Stories*, a book of short stories. Both collections were intended for young readers. *Baseball in April and Other Stories* won the American Library Association's Best Book for Young Adults award. Comprised of eleven short stories, it deals with the pitfalls, triumphs, joys, devastations, and challenges of being a Latino teenager in California's Central Valley. Some of the trials endured by these teens are universal to all North American adolescents, including Little League tryouts, attraction to the opposite sex, and embarrassing grandparents. The book was well received by critics who particularly praised Soto's insight into the emotional world of children and the universality of teenagers' concerns, regardless of whatever cultural differences separate them.

Soto's momentum as a young adult author continued to rise in 1991, with the publication of the young adult novel *Taking Sides* and a collection of essays and stories titled *A Summer Life*. *Taking Sides* concerned eighth grader Lincoln Mendoza, who has just moved with his mother from a Hispanic neighborhood in San Francisco to a wealthy, mostly white suburb. A talented basketball player, Lincoln now plays for the arch-rival of his old school, creating a sense of divided loyalties. Lincoln feels like a traitor to his old school and his old friends, but he also feels rejected by his new coach and teammates. Gradually, the plot moves toward the big game between Lincoln's new and old schools and a resolution that allows Lincoln to happily bridge both worlds.

A Summer Life is a collection of thirty-nine essays and short stories that delve into Soto's most cherished memories of his childhood in Fresno. He lovingly details the little things that once made up his entire world—his tennis sneakers that smelled of grass, asphalt, and sweat socks; his dress shoes that tapped and sparked on the sidewalks; and a cherished Buddha statue flecked with gold paint.

In the following year, Soto issued a volume of poetry titled *Neighborhood Odes*. This work also celebrated the everyday magic of neighborhood life, such as playing in sprinklers, awaiting the arrival of the ice-cream truck, eating snow cones, playing the guitar, watching fireworks, going on picnics, and visiting the library. Soto followed *A Summer Life* in 1993 with a collection of stories titled *Local News*. Closer in spirit to *Baseball in April and Other Stories*, this collection presents thirteen tales about the daily troubles and triumphs of Latino adolescents in California. The story plots range from a girl's dream of flying and her scary and disappointing first plane ride ("Nickel-a-Pound Plane Ride") to a yard work job that goes awry when a pile of raked leaves starts to burn out of control ("First Job"). "Blackmail," another story in the collection, represents something of a departure for Soto. In it he portrays siblings who, far from pulling together to support and protect each other, actually act more like enemies. One day when Angel is taking a shower, his older brother Javier sneaks into the bathroom and takes a picture of him naked. Javier then threatens to show the picture to all the girls at school if Angel does not pay him twenty dollars. When Angel is unable to produce the money, Javier forces him to do his chores instead.

In most of Soto's stories and novels, the characters' siblings and other family members help protect them from this kind of meanness, which is usually coming from a classmate or neighborhood bully. Families are usually safe havens, which is why Angel's situation is so horrifying. He cannot even count on his brother for love and support.

Soto's next young adult novel, *Pacific Crossing* (1992), was also something of a departure. Although it centers on two Mexican American boys from California, the usual setting for a Soto novel—a Hispanic neighborhood in East Los Angeles, Fresno, or San Francisco—changes radically. This story takes readers to Japan. The tale finds Lincoln and Tony, who have just started to practice the martial art of kempo, heading to Japan as part of an exchange program. Once there, they live with a host family, work in the fields, and practice kempo. Initially feeling like fish out of water, the boys eventually come to love and appreciate the host country as they discover the universality of family and friendships. They soon learn that Japan, its people, and its families are not so very different from the world they have temporarily left behind.

A Fertile Period

With the same tireless energy he expended in the grape and cotton fields around Fresno, Soto continued to write, publish more books, and work on other creative projects. More awards and praise followed. Between 1991 and 1994, Soto wrote, produced, and directed three short films, one of which, *The Pool Party*, won the Andrew Carnegie Medal. In 1994, he also published a novel for young adults titled *Jesse*. The book centers on a seventeen-year-old Mexican American boy who, during the late 1960s, is struggling with an alcoholic stepfather, confusion about the war in Vietnam, and the danger of giving in to either poverty or the draft. The parallels with Soto's own background are clear. Joel Shoemaker, writing in *School Library Journal* in 1994, called Jesse's story "poignant, pregnant with unfulfilled promise and dreams of a future that is hoped for but rarely imagined. Simple words reveal universal experiences."[1] Perhaps because of its similarity to the events of his own youth, *Jesse* is Soto's favorite among the books he has written.

The year 1994 also saw the publication of *Crazy Weekend*, another young adult novel. Just as its title suggests, the book centers on one very action-packed and comical weekend that two East Los Angeles teenagers spend in Fresno. Hector and his best friend, Mando, are visiting

Hector's uncle Julio. When Julio takes them up in a plane to take aerial photographs of local farms, they witness and photograph an armored car heist. Back on the ground, Mando and Hector foolishly boast to a local newspaper journalist about their role in gathering evidence of the crime. As a result, the armored car robbers hear about the teens and begin to pursue them. The wild plot comes to a suspenseful and hilarious conclusion in Uncle Julio's apartment. One reviewer described the adventure story as a cross between the movies *Home Alone* and Alfred Hitchcock's *Rear Window*. Hector and Mando proved popular enough with readers for Soto to bring them back in 1995's *Summer on Wheels*. An episodic novel, the story follows the two teens on an eight-day bike ride from East Los Angeles to Santa Monica, fueled mostly by junk food. During their trek, they visit and stay with relatives and experience a string of adventures and misadventures.

Becoming a Full-time Writer

Although he continued to teach during this busy period of artistic production and critical praise, Soto was growing tired of Berkeley's lack of commitment to hiring more minorities for the faculty. As a result, he felt it was time to quit and write full-time. In his essay "Getting It Done," he writes about this decision in 1995 to resign and walk away from his teaching job.

> The end of my teaching career began suddenly when, during a faculty meeting, the faces of my colleagues underwent a frightening metamorphosis. They began to resemble various chicken parts—breast, thighs, wings—muffled behind the sheen of Saran Wrap . . . That was the beginning of the end for me, and two years later, after other surrealistic hot flashes and dark cloudlike drifts of depression, I quit teaching altogether. After my last class, I literally jogged off the Cal Berkeley campus, arms hugging bundles of teaching evaluations after thirteen years of rubbing my bottom on hard chairs. Happy that my books were selling, I took the beautifully redneck stance of, "Take this job and shove it!"[2]

One of the first tasks Soto set himself to after leaving the university was turning his garage into a study for writing. Now that he was working full-time on his stories, poems, and essays, he began to produce even more. In 1997, he wrote a story called "The No-Guitar Blues" for Anita Silvey's *Help Wanted: Short Stories About Young People Working*. In it, the main character is a young man named Fausto. He finds a less-than-honest way to raise the money he needs to buy a used guitar, but then finds that his conscience will not let him keep it. Instead, he donates the money to his church, thus regaining peace of mind. His story of guilt and redemption is one that teens of all backgrounds understand. Recently, "The No-Guitar Blues" was made into a short film of the same name.

Darker Themes

Another one of Soto's young adult novels is called *Buried Onions* (1997). It is a story that does not pull any punches or try to provide some kind of artificially happy ending. The main character is a nineteen-year-old Mexican American named Eddie. The title is derived from the fact that Eddie always smells onions in the air of his hometown. He associates such smells with feelings of hopelessness and despair. "I had a theory about those vapors," Eddie muses, "which were not released by the sun's heat but by a huge onion buried under the city. This onion made us cry. Tears leapt from our eyelashes and stained our faces."[3]

Eddie's life is extremely difficult, as gang violence, drugs, addiction, poverty, and murder surround him. He describes his environment in stark terms, saying, "I returned to my apartment, which was in a part of Fresno where fences sagged and the paint blistered on houses ... Laundry wept from the lines, the faded flags of the poor, ignorant, unemployable people."[4] Eddie tries to find ways to rise above his life. In the end, he joins the military, seeing it as his best—his only—hope of survival.

In 1999, Soto won the Literature Award from the Hispanic Heritage Foundation and the Author-Illustrator Civil Rights Award from the National Education Association. In addition, he won the PEN Center West Book Award for his book *Petty Crimes* (1998). This last collection was made up of ten short stories about a variety of Mexican American teenagers who learn valuable life lessons as they interact with family, friends, and enemies. Through their sometimes funny, sometimes painful experiences, these teens develop character and learn how to use their bodies and minds for good purposes. Critics praised the stories for their realism, for their unblinking focus on these young people's daily concerns regarding poverty, gang violence, and crime, as well as the more mundane but no less urgent worries of adolescence.

Soto returned to adult fiction in 2000 with *Nickel and Dime*. In it, he tells the story of three desperate men dealing with poverty, the death of dreams, and a pervasive disappointment with life. Once again, Soto received rave reviews. The *School Library Journal* compared *Nickel and Dime* to the works of classic authors such as John Steinbeck. The *New York Times* praised the book for its power and brutal honesty.

In 2001, Soto continued his return to adult fiction by issuing *Poetry Lover*, a novel that served as a sequel to *Nickel and Dime*. It is another of his favorites. The character of homeless poet Silver Mendez is featured in both of the books. In *Poetry Lover*, a sense of hope returns to Mendez's life through new professional opportunities and romantic involvement. Reviewers praised Soto for compassionately illuminating the struggle some artists engage in to keep their creative souls alive and protected against the onslaught of poverty and discrimination. Silver Mendez would return once more in Soto's *Amnesia in a Republican County* (2003).

One of Soto's most unusual works was published in 2003. The young adult novel *The Afterlife* is the story of a seventeen-year-old Chicano named Chuy. In a daring and unusual move on Soto's part, Chuy is killed on the second page of the book. While standing in the bathroom of a local music spot called Club Estrella, Chuy comments on the yellow shoes of the guy standing next to him. Misunderstanding what was intended to be a simple compliment, the other man is angered and sticks a knife in Chuy's chest. It is a fatal blow, and Chuy recognizes this immediately.

> I pillowed my head on my arm, moaned. The floor was cold and dirty, with tracks of shoe prints. It was the territory of mice and cockroaches, but I was neither. I closed my eyes. When I opened them a minute later, I was dead.[5]

Throughout the rest of the book, the ghost of Chuy discovers things he had not realized before about his friends and family, such as just how fiercely they loved and cared for him. As a ghost, he also manages to save a life, punish a thug, and fall in love with the ghost of a girl who committed suicide. All the while, Chuy's ghost body is dissolving limb by limb, as his connection to life weakens.

Gary Soto's interest in writing about childhood, family, neighborhoods, best friends, animals, and food—among many other things—makes him a favorite author among teen readers. Soto has also developed a loyal following among younger children through the publication of his many picture books. The same rich and vibrant world Soto creates in his writings for adults and young adults comes to even more colorful life in the pages of his sweet and funny storybooks.

4 Stories for Younger Readers

Although Gary Soto has written many novels for adults and young adults, he has also contributed a great deal to the world of children's picture books. These lighthearted, delightful stories focus more on life's joys than do some of his darker works for older readers. Because of the sense of wonder and excitement conveyed in these picture books, it comes as little surprise that some of Soto's biggest fans are also his smallest ones.

As in his other novels, stories, and essays, Soto creates main characters in all of his picture books who are Mexican American. Whether it is a little boy excited to discover that he looks like his papi or a cool cat determined to throw the neighborhood's best party, each story subtly reveals Soto's pride and respect for his ethnic heritage.

The Coolest Cat

In 1995, Soto penned *Chato's Kitchen*, a lighthearted story for three- to eight-year-olds about Chato, the coolest cat in East Los Angeles, and his favorite buddy, Novio Boy. When a family of mice moves in next door, the two felines invite them over for a dinner of Mexican specialties. However, they are really planning to make the rodents the main dish on the menu. When the mice bring some unusual sausage to eat instead, the dinner party goes in unexpected directions. The book won the Parent's Choice Award, as well as an American Library Association Notable Book Award.

The character of Chato was such a beloved one that five years later, in 2000, Soto wrote a sequel called *Chato and the Party Animals*. When the cool cat discovers that his best friend, Novio Boy, has never had a real birthday party—a *pachanga*—Chato sets out to fix that by throwing him the best party ever. He arranges for the cake, music, and, of course, the piñata. The one thing he forgets to do is invite Novio Boy to his own birthday party! Ann Welton from *School Library Journal* called the book, "a joyous celebration of friendship . . . Irresistible."[1] Other reviewers praised the Chato books for their expressive animal drawings—by Susan Guevara—and lively compositions. Additional Chato stories are in the works, including *Chato Goes Cruisin'* and *Chato's Day of Dead*, both due to be published in 2005.

Celebrating Family and Dealing with Loss

In 1998, Soto wrote another picture book for young readers called *Big Bushy Mustache*. In it, he tells the story of a determined little boy named Ricky, who is preparing to play a Mexican soldier in his class's upcoming play about the Chicano holiday Cinco de Mayo. The holiday celebrates the Mexican victory over French invaders on May 5, 1862. Ricky is offered a range of props to use or wear on stage. He turns down a sword, pistol, cape, and even a sombrero, for the prop he wants most is a big, black mustache called a *bigote*. Part of his interest in the bigote is that his father sports a real one just like it. Ricky is tired of hearing how much he looks like his mother and would rather be told that he looks manly like his father. When Ricky loses the mustache on the way home from school, it is up to him and his father to find a replacement.

As in *Big Bushy Mustache*, Soto's picture books are often concerned with the theme of losing something that is precious to the main character or one of his or her family members. The search for what is lost often draws friends and family closer together in a time of crisis. In the book *Too Many Tamales* (1993), a young girl named Maria tries on her mother's wedding ring while making tamales for the family Christmas celebration. She is stricken with fear later when she cannot find the ring. She and her cousins band together to search for the missing jewelry by eating all of the two dozen tamales. As the children bond during their effort to help Maria, Soto reveals the special closeness and strength of family.

A book with a similar theme is *The Skirt* (1994). Its main character is a young girl named Miata Ramirez who has recently moved with her family from an apartment in Los Angeles to a house in Sanger, a small town in the San

Joaquin Valley. Miata sometimes tends to forget things and then gets into trouble. When she accidentally leaves her folklorico skirt—a traditional Mexican costume—on the school bus one Friday afternoon, she panics because she needs to wear it for a folk dance celebration at church that Sunday. Worse yet, the skirt once belonged to her mother when she was a child in Mexico, and the garment is now an important family heirloom. As a result, Miata and her best friend, Ana, have to break into the school bus to retrieve the skirt before her parents find out. Ann Welton from *School Library Journal* described *The Skirt* as, "a light, engaging narrative that successfully combines information on Hispanic culture with familiar and recognizable childhood themes."[2]

Another Soto picture book that features a cherished article of clothing is *If the Shoe Fits*, published in 2002. It tells the story of Rigo, the youngest child in a family, who is tired of wearing his brothers' worn-out and frayed hand-me-downs. He is delighted when given a brand-new pair of penny loafers—the very first new article of clothing that was bought just for him. Unfortunately, other kids on the playground make fun of his new shoes and steal the pennies he has slid inside the slots on the loafer's tongues. Now embarrassed by his new shoes, Rigo puts them away and refuses to wear them.

A few months later, when getting ready for a party, he wants to wear dress shoes and takes out the loafers again, only to find that they no longer fit. Luckily, his uncle is about to begin a new job as a waiter and needs a good pair of shoes. Rigo is finally in a position to hand something down to someone else, and his uncle gladly accepts the loafers. In return, Rigo is given an old pair of his uncle's shoes from Mexico. Through this exchange, Rigo learns the true value of things that are old and passed down through the family. In the process, he also sees that being part of a big, supportive, and sharing family can be very helpful and a great advantage.

Soto's interest in families is not limited to only children's roles within them. He also writes about the funny situations that parents can get themselves into. *The Old Man and His Door* (1996) highlights a problem common to almost all families, regardless of ethnic background: husbands who do not listen very carefully to their wives. Although the main character of this novel—the Old Man—can grow the best hot chili peppers in the neighborhood, and raise pigs "as plump as water balloons," he tends not to hear what his wife tells him. When she asks him to bring *el puerco*, the pig, to the nearby barbecue, the silly man brings *la puerta*, the door of his house, instead. On his way to the party, with la puerta carried on his back, the Old Man discovers many original uses for a door. In *The Old Man and His Door*, Soto is playing with old folktales, particularly the "wise fool" stories in which a character's silly or foolish actions allow listeners to laugh at their own mistakes and awkward moments while also teaching some simple homespun wisdom.

Given that family and communal celebrations are so central to many of Soto's stories, it was inevitable that he would eventually focus on a wedding ceremony in one of them. In *Snapshots from a Wedding* (1997), Soto provides the reader with a vivid description of a Chicano wedding ceremony and celebration. The narrator of the story is flower girl Maya, who sneaks black olives on to each of her fingers at the reception when no one is looking. Her description of the wedding party emerges from the "snapshot" images she recalls—the dancing, the wedding cake, the mariachi band (a group of Mexican street musicians).

Due to his restless creativity and desire to speak to as many people as possible through his writing, it is no surprise that Gary Soto has also mastered the difficult art of poetry. Indeed, all of these images of family, friendship, food, fun, and favorite possessions found in his prose work for children, teens, and adults come to even more vibrant life in Soto's poetry.

5 Soto's Poetry

It was the words of many of the world's best poets—including Edward Field, W. S. Merwin, Charles Simic, James Wright, and Pablo Neruda—that first inspired Gary Soto to put pen to paper during college. It comes as little surprise, then, that his earliest attempts at writing were poems, and verse remains one of his favorite forms. Similar to the work of Shel Silverstein, author of *The Giving Tree* and *Where the Sidewalk Ends*, Soto's poetry speaks to readers of all ages, backgrounds, and life experiences. The small child chuckles at his words just as the adult sighs over a nostalgic moment movingly remembered and described. As with everything else he writes, Soto's poetry speaks to the universal humanity that is contained within each person.

Early Poems

Along with his many other achievements, Gary Soto is also one of the youngest poets ever to be included in the *Norton Anthology of Modern Poetry*, a prestigious collection of the best work of some of the most respected and talented poets writing in English. Three of Soto's poems that appear in the *Norton Anthology* are among his earliest published works. Intended primarily for adults, the poems deviate from Soto's usual concerns with family, children, parents, music, and food. Instead, they are devoted to a close observation of nature and the way the human body experiences and interacts with the natural world.

The first of these poems, "Wind (2)" (1977) describes a blazing hot morning that suddenly yields to a cold wind and gray clouds. It is so hot in the morning that even a lizard blinks against the brightness and must seek shelter under some leaves. Although the beating sun seems relentless, the cold wind that follows is no less penetrating. It is so bracing and strong that it instantly pierces through the body and exits as quickly, expelled in a sort of chill-induced hyperventilation: "And the cold wind you breathed/ Was moving under your skin and already far/ From the small hives of your lungs."[1] This is no idyllic vision of nature, with babbling brooks and pretty meadows. Rather, the desert landscape is subject to extremes of weather that test the endurance of animals and humans alike. The natural world is as brutal as it is invigorating and beautiful.

The second poem reproduced in the *Norton Anthology*, "Rain" (1977), is more directly concerned with the perspective of the speaker rather than nature. Yet the speaker's fortunes are revealed to be intimately bound up with the natural world and the cycle of seasons. The speaker seems to be a migrant worker who is thinking about the coming of the autumn rains. With the arrival of fall, the speaker realizes he will be out of work. Just as the anthill homes of the relentlessly busy ants will be flattened by the rains, so, too, will the speaker's life be reduced by unemployment. Without any money, he will have no occasion to wear his good slacks, which will gather lint in the closet. His plates and silverware will go unused due to lack of food. Hunger will set in: "The skin of my belly will tighten like a belt/ And there will be no reason for pockets."[2] Once again, Soto depicts the forces and cycles of nature as harsh, extreme, and even cruel.

Whereas the arrival of autumn rain represents the change from a season of work and plenty to a period of unemployment and hunger in "Rain," the lack of rain also signals even greater hunger and catastrophe in "Drought" (1978), a third nature poem by Soto collected in the *Norton Anthology*. Though clouds climb up and over the mountains, they refuse to release their load of moisture when they descend into the parched, deserted valley. The drought has created a broken, barren landscape in which even sound seems to have ceased. Shingles of slate have cracked from the heat and dryness. Roads have become untraveled. The doors of abandoned houses swing open and closed, and the broken windows let in the dusty wind. All of nature has gone bony with hunger. The trees are "dried thin as hat racks." The wind "plucks the birds spineless." The young people who leave the area to search for relief and a better life carry "a few seeds in each pocket,/ Their belts tightened on the fifth notch of hunger."[3] All of nature has grown silent, maintaining a desperate vigil for a change of weather. Bottles in abandoned cellars have "held their breath for years," and even the sky itself is "deafened from listening for rain."[4]

Skinny Poems

Soto's early poems were intended primarily for an adult audience, although their simple, straightforward language and concrete imagery make them accessible to younger readers as well. Yet Soto also writes poetry designed especially for his younger audience. With his typical good humor, Soto says that he once thought he had to write the same way he looked. "I weighed 115 pounds," he chuckles, "and so I wrote skinny poems."[5] A good example of one of his "skinny poems" is found in *Canto Familiar*, an illustrated collection of poems about the pain and pleasure of growing up Mexican American, published in 1995. "Papi's Menudo" manages to pack an amazing amount of rich sensory language into a very skinny and relatively brief poem. Soto makes you feel as if you are right there in Papi's house eating *menudo*, a fragrant soup made of tripe (the stomach tissue of an ox or cow), hominy (washed and stripped corn kernels), and chili. It is stewed for hours with garlic and other spices, creating a rich, red, fatty broth that is thought to stimulate the senses and the appetite, soothe the stomach, and clear the head. It is usually served in big open bowls.

Papi's Menudo

It's served
On Sunday,
Just as Papi
Wakes with
Red in his eyes
And whiskers
The color
Of iron filings
Standing up
On a magnet.
It comes in
A yellow pot,
A curl of steam
Unraveling
When you lift
The lid and look in:
Tripas wagging
Like tongues
On the bottom
When you take
A spoon and stir,
Stir, dip,
And stir. Sunday
Steam fogs the kitchen
Window, the Mexican

Station is
Starting up
Its eight violins.
Papi could cry
From the whine
Of these violins,
But it's too early.
Papi leans over
The table and
Runs a hand
Over his sleepy face.
When Mami sets
A bowl in front
Of him, he sits up
Like a good boy.
He squeezes
The lemon until
It collapses
Like a clown's frown.
He sprinkles
His *menudo* with onion
And rubs oregano
Between his lucky palms.
He roars, *Que rico!*
He lifts his spoon
And blows. He
Slurps and hisses,
A slither of *tripas*
Riding down the
Chute of his throat.
He tears a piece

Of tortilla
And dips into his *menudo*,
Medicine on Sunday
When he worked
With both hands
On Saturday. Now
It's morning.
I sit next
To my bear of
A father. When
He slurps,
I slurp, stirring
Awake the whiskers
Of my cat, Hambre.
His greedy cat eyes
Spring open,
And he leaps
To his feet,
Nudging first
My legs, then Papi's,
Meowing for the love of tortilla
Dipped three times in *menudo*.[6]

Although Soto vividly describes the delicious Sunday meal as intensely pleasurable, he characteristically injects a few sad notes of realism. Life for Papi is not easy, and this relaxing and delicious meal is perhaps a rare pleasure. Indeed, the menudo is described as a "medicine," a cure for the hard manual labor of the previous day. And the Mexican music playing on the radio is not simply a pleasant diversion, but a sound so heavy with memory and longing that it can provoke exhausted Papi's tears.

As with his picture books, however, Soto disperses any dark clouds with images of warmth, love, and family. Father and son share the pleasure of the menudo together, and the son is happy and proud to be sitting next to his father, learning from him, and imitating his actions. Animals are also important to many of Soto's stories, and in this poem the family cat provides a sweet conclusion. As father and son bond over breakfast, the cat—a full-fledged member of the family—begs to be included in the cozy meal.

The Music of Poetry

Many of these same elements—family, music, food, and the family cat—appear in another poem from *Canto Familiar*, titled "Music for Fun and Profit." The speaker of this poem is madly in love with music and uses whatever is handy to help coax the sounds in his head out into the wider world. A sort of one-man band, he makes a wide array of instruments out of common household items: an oatmeal box becomes a drum, a comb covered in waxed paper doubles as a harmonica, a straw serves as a flute, and a coat hanger becomes a makeshift triangle. A shoe box and fishing line make a primitive guitar, pie tins serve as cymbals, and soup cans filled with BBs become maracas. He even uses his own body to create a multitude of sounds—slapping his thighs, whistling through his nose, and noisily blowing through puffed-out cheeks to create rhythm and melody. The boy's musical repertoire is impressively wide and varied, from spirituals like "Michael Row the Boat Ashore" and traditional Mexican songs to showtunes ("Old Man River") and the rock 'n' roll classic "Louie, Louie."

The fun of music-making is delightfully evoked in "Music for Fun and Profit." But where does the profit come in? It turns out that not everyone enjoys the speaker's music as much as he does himself. The constant drumming of his fork and spoon on the kitchen table upsets his parents. Even his cool "low-riding" cat seems unimpressed by the boy's attempt to serenade him. While his father tries to read the newspaper in the living room, the speaker trots out one of his homemade instruments and begins to strike up a tune. What sounds like sweet music to the boy is just noise to his father. To gain a little peace and quiet, the father fishes in his pockets for change and pays his son to stop playing his music. So making music is fun, and not playing it is profitable! As the boy runs off with his pockets full of money, the coins make a different sort of music as they jangle together.

Once again, this sweet and warm poem includes some dark undertones. For example, the boy makes his own instruments because the family cannot afford to buy real ones. Plus, the boy's parents get angry with him when he buys a two-dollar kazoo. To them, it seems like a waste of precious money.

Fearless Fernie

One of Soto's most ambitious poetic undertakings is *Fearless Fernie: Hanging Out with Fernie and Me*, published in 2002. It is a collection of forty-one linked poems that, taken together, recount the friendship between the narrator and his best friend, Fernie, from infancy through early adolescence and middle school. Reading the poems in this collection is like looking through a rich, moving, and funny scrapbook of two friends' shared memories.

From their initial meeting as babies, Fernie and the narrator quickly become and remain best buddies, even through the many ups and downs of childhood, school pressures, social embarrassments, and romance. With these poems, Soto returns to the themes of his other writing for young people—family, friendship, romance, school, dances, dates, and social interaction. Most are humorous and sweet, though occasionally darkened by Soto's trademark realism.

Two poems in *Fearless Fernie* concern an obsession typical among middle-school boys—sports. In the first, "How Coach Told Me I Didn't Make the Cut," the narrator eagerly follows his football coach's order to go out for a pass. Heading downfield, dreaming of glory and success, he continuously looks back, only to see his coach still holding on to the ball and shouting to run farther still. Eventually, the narrator runs so far that the coach is just a dot on the horizon. The boy stops running and realizes that this was the coach's way of cutting him from the squad.

Arriving home to an empty living room, he watches television and sees cheering crowds. He imagines they are cheering for his classmates who made the team. As funny as the situation is—going long for a pass that is never thrown—the poem is suffused with sadness as the boy is separated from the team and ends up alone, on the outside of things. He feels the pain all young people experience—the pain of not getting what you want, no matter how hard you try.

"Fall Football," the second poem about sports in the *Fearless Fernie* collection, continues the boy's story. Having been cut from the football team, the narrator is forced to play alone and imagine a team around him in a fully fleshed out, dramatic game. Only the boy's faithful cat is present to witness his heroic exploits on the playing field, as he chases his own passes and tumbles across his lawn. After his imaginary team takes the lead 14–0, the game comes to an abrupt end when the porch light turns on, signaling dinnertime. In a locker room interview afterward, the boy asks himself about the game. Rubbing a sore shoulder, he replies to himself, "'It was a personal challenge,' I said, exhausted./ 'It's always hard when I play against myself.'"[7] Once again, an amusing premise—the imaginary backyard heroics of a non-athlete—is shaded by the sadness and loneliness of solitary play.

A similar instance of a humorous and imaginative revision of reality that disguises darker emotions is at the center of "King Kong Versus Me." In it, the narrator recounts a fight he had with King Kong (perhaps representing some big, hairy enemy at school). He repeatedly states that he took a step, and the reader assumes he moved closer and closer toward his enemy. The narrator expresses the great anger he felt, claiming that his eyes brimmed with fire, his nostrils streamed smoke, and his fists were balled and ready to strike. Yet just as the narrator seems to reach a fever pitch of rage, a sudden reversal occurs. The storyteller claims that he and his opponent never ended up fighting. Instead, readers learn that King Kong was the one moving toward the narrator in a threatening way. All the steps the narrator was taking were away from his enemy, not toward him. So what initially seems to be a tale of heroism and righteous anger turns out to be one of fear and retreat. Like any child who loses or runs away from a fight, the narrator wishes to save face with his peers and with himself. As a result, he recasts the events in a more exaggerated and favorable way, using humor and monster movie imagery to distract readers from his fear of fighting.

Soto's Poetry

The sadness that lurks beneath the surface of these poems comes right to the surface in "Guilt." In it, the narrator's best friend, Fernie, is in bed remembering his third-grade friends and the great times they had together. After reminiscing about the group's playground exploits, joyful run-ins with sprinklers, and love of Popsicles, Fernie finds his thoughts suddenly veering off in a very different direction. His own memory of good times somehow reminds him of a third grader who knew no such happiness. Fernie's classmate had no friends and ate lunch alone at the far corner of the playground during recess. His only companions were some sparrows who gathered around him to eat bits of the dry sandwich he offered them. Fernie, stricken with guilt for not befriending the boy, wonders if his classmate is still there, frozen in his solitude. Fernie wonders if the sparrows still keep him company, or "did they fly elsewhere/ Once the boy—what's his name—had nothing to give,/ His lunch all gone, loneliness like crumbs at his feet."[8]

Soto's poems for young readers are often concerned with the desire to appear heroic and save the day. Often this desire is prompted by humiliation, like getting cut from the football team, running away from a fight, or being excluded from the activities of classmates. In "Orange Socks," also from *Fearless Fernie*, the narrator survives the ridicule of his classmates at a school dance and eventually rescues them during a blackout later that night. Because his family's washer seems to eat all of his dark socks, the narrator is forced to wear a bright orange pair to the dance, messing up his otherwise cool outfit of black pants, white shirt, and shiny black shoes. The socks provoke general hilarity, as girls run away from the narrator in horror, boys spit ice cubes at him, and teachers take up a collection for him to buy dark socks. Sidelined by this ridicule, the narrator sits by a window and talks to himself. Suddenly the lights go out and chaos reigns. As people try to exit the school building, they slip on the ice cubes that had earlier been spat at the narrator. They also slide on the small change the teachers have collected for him. Finally recognizing the value of his bright orange socks, the narrator orders everyone to form a chain behind him and follow the glow of his socks out of the building. Once mocked, the narrator is now hailed as a hero.

Even if one is able to win over his or her classmates, there is always the adult world to conquer. While Soto usually depicts family life as warm and supportive, with loving if stern parents, the adults one encounters outside of the family can often provoke fear, anger, hurt, or sadness. In "On the Escalator at Macy's," the narrator of *Fearless Fernie* encounters a sour woman in the department store. She seems to hate him simply because of his undone shoelaces, his torn T-shirt, or some other aspect of his appearance. The more the narrator tries to be polite and friendly, the more hateful she becomes. Finally, without any provocation, she mutters, "I'm glad I don't have kids!"[9] As much as the narrator tries to put the incident behind him, he cannot help but view the woman's grumpy mouth as a mousetrap, snapping shut on "kids like me, mouselike, trying to wiggle out of her bite."[10]

One reason that Soto's poetry appeals so much to a young audience is because it reads less like poetry and more like carefully worded snapshots of real life in its funny, embarrassing, poignant, tragic, and mundane moments. The most unique aspect of these word snapshots, however, is that although readers may not know the photographer or some of the people in the photo, they certainly imagine themselves being in the middle of the same situation. As Mary T.

Garrote observed in *School Library Journal*, "Whether [Soto] is reliving a trip to the cemetery, a shopping excursion to the local market, or the nostalgia days of black-and-white TV, he presents each word [of poetry], each line with power. Soto's language is spare and plain like the people and places he describes."[11]

6 Seeing Soto's Stories

Along with his picture books, novels, short stories, poems, and essays, Gary Soto has also penned a couple of plays and biographies. In *Novio Boy: A Play* (1997), Soto tells the story of Rudy, a ninth grader who finds the courage to ask Patricia, an eleventh grader, out on a date. Against all odds, she accepts. Most of the play's action is devoted to Rudy's desperate seeking of the money, advice, conversational tips, and self-confidence he will need to make the date a success. The hilarious events of the date itself are also revealed.

Soto's second play is called *Nerdlandia* (1999). The story centers on a character named

Martin, a Chicano nerd, complete with glasses, calculator, and high-waisted pants. In an attempt to win over the girl he loves, Martin, with the help of his friends, transforms himself into a much "cooler" guy. While Martin works to make himself a little cooler, however, the girl he loves learns to be a bit more nerdy. Many critics have described this sweet and funny play as a Chicano version of *Grease*. For the Los Angeles Opera, Soto wrote a libretto for an opera based on the play, which was also titled *Nerdlandia*.

Soto's Biographies

Always seeking new and creative ways to examine, celebrate, and honor his ethnic heritage, Gary Soto has occasionally looked beyond fiction and memoir. He has written two biographies of important Chicano activists for young readers. *Jessie de la Cruz: A Profile of a United Farm Worker* (2000) introduces the reader to one of the most important organizers of Chicano agricultural laborers. The first female organizer of the United Farm Workers, she encouraged the laborers to stand up for their rights, learn how to conduct a strike for higher pay and better working conditions, and join together in a union to work toward common goals.

The United Farm Workers is a union of farm workers—including immigrant migrant laborers—started by Cesar Chavez and Dolores Huerta in the mid-1960s. Chavez, Huerta, and de la Cruz were among the most influential and passionate champions of exploited migrant agricultural laborers and helped gain wage increases, better working conditions, and greater worker safety for the nation's farmworkers, especially in California. Soto met de la Cruz at a gathering of the California Rural Assistance League in 1988. Shortly thereafter, he decided to write a book about her life and accomplishments. Soto details the work of de la Cruz and her husband over the course of more than half a century.

Three years later, Soto issued *Cesar Chavez: A Hero for Everyone* for third to fifth graders. In it, he follows the labor leader's life from his childhood in Arizona, to his teen years as a migrant laborer, his efforts to help fellow farm workers organize for their rights, and his founding of the United Farm Workers.

In the early 2000s, Soto has continued to write for adult and teen readers, but he has also found other ways to support and celebrate his Mexican heritage. He is a frequent and popular speaker at conferences, and his essays, stories, and poems continue to appear in a variety of magazines. He serves as a judge for a number of literary contests and has edited the Chicano Chapbook Series, which attempted to call attention to emerging Latino and Latina writers. He is the Young People Ambassador for the California Rural Legal Assistance (CRLA) and the United Farm Workers of America (UFW). CRLA offers financial and legal help to the state's rural poor, often by providing them with the services of a lawyer for free or at a low cost.

A Writer's Life

Today, Soto keeps busy by working on a variety of projects. His usual schedule is to write from 8:30 AM until noon at his house in Berkeley, California, where he lives with his wife Carolyn, their daughter, Mariko, and several cats. His afternoons are devoted to answering some of the large amounts of mail he receives every day. Soto aims to produce three to four pages of text a day and a chapter every two weeks. Most of his writing is done in bed with a laptop.

Following the morning's mental workout of writing, he frequently spends time exercising his body through the Japanese martial arts of aikido and tae kwon do. In fact, Soto has already achieved a black belt in tae kwon do. He also enjoys Aztec dancing and playing basketball. Soto, who finds time to teach English at his local church, believes that literacy is an important cause. Part of the reason he turned his attention to children's literature was his hope that if he could reach young people with his stories, he could turn them into readers and writers, just as he had been inspired to write in college following his discovery of poetry.

Evenings are spent with his family, either at home or eating out at new restaurants. Much time is also devoted to reading. "It appears these days I don't have much of a life because my nose is often stuck [in] a book," Soto writes on his Web site. "But I discovered that reading builds a life inside the mind."[1]

In his interview with Scholastic.com, Soto sums up his feelings about his writing in this way: "To me the finest praise is when a reader says, I can see your stories. This is what I'm always working for, a story that becomes alive and meaningful in the reader's mind. That's why I write so much about growing up in the barrio. It allows me to use specific memories that are vivid for me."[2]

Gary Soto would like every reader to be able to "see" his stories. Whether he is delighting young readers with a picture book celebrating

Mexican American life and the joys and sorrows of childhood or presenting a play that makes both actors and audiences cringe and laugh simultaneously, Gary Soto stays true to his ideal of taking pride in one's cultural heritage and truthfully presenting life as it is. In every one of the many books he has written, Soto continues to prove his ability to describe and relate to young people's emotions, battles, and amazing adventures.

Interview with Gary Soto

Tamra Orr: Unlike many authors, you did not begin writing until you were in college, first at Fresno City College and then at Cal State, Fresno. What do you think was the primary reason you discovered the pleasure of writing at that particular age or in these particular places?

Gary Soto: In truth I dabbled at writing in high school in part because of the heady music of the time—Bob Dylan, Donovan, the Beatles, some of the Rolling Stones—and I believed then, and still do, that writing was a shining path. I felt like a poet then but didn't do anything about it until later. I started writing at Fresno State College because I had suppressed emotions that had to come out, namely the death of my father, and secondly, the turmoil of my home life. Also, at that time, the role of the writer—poet or novelist—was a supreme position for evaluating your life. A person could become a doctor, a lawyer, a politician, a gardener, but very few could say that they wrote poetry. I was willing to take this chance, even if it meant poverty.

Tamra Orr: Do you think that you would have taken to writing with such sustained passion and energy if you had started at a younger age? Do you think your writing would have been different in any important way had you started at an earlier age?

Gary Soto: There are few writers whose juvenilia are worth reading. Most writers begin their serious work in their mid-twenties, though there are some whose work doesn't happen until much later. I'm thinking of Robert Frost. He didn't really start until he was in his forties; that is, success didn't happen to him until then. Then there is Olive Ann Burns, author of *Cold Sassy Tree*, who didn't start until, I believe, her seventies. In short, I can't imagine anyone starting in their teens whose work was memorable—I can hear others saying, "There's the *Diary of Anne Frank*." Yes, of course, but this is a tragic exception. Second, I do believe writers have a time span in which they have a sustained power of language and creativity. How much do we really expect from our creative minds?

Tamra Orr: Other than the sheer love of storytelling, what is it that makes you want to write? What is it about the process or the result that is so enjoyable and gratifying?

Gary Soto: I enjoy the laughter. I wrote three adults novels during which I thought I was the funniest guy on the face of our dirty planet. Writers need to feel something. We're not a machine. I need laughter, I need tears, I need that feeling of arrival when I come to the close of a poem, an essay, a novel, or any other form of writing. It's like cutting the lawn; I want it done and done well.

Tamra Orr: You have written poetry, picture books, short stories, biographies, essays, plays, and novels for both young adults and adults. Do you have a favorite genre? Is there one that is your first love or that comes more easily to you?

Gary Soto: At heart I'm a poet, and I suspect poetry writing is truer than any of the other genres. During my early years of writing during the 1970s, I woke to poetry, walked with poetry, and went to bed with poetry. I was charmed by its beauty and mesmerized by its mystery. I didn't quite get everything I read, but I realized that men and women poets from another time were trying to tell me something. I think I was a good listener.

Tamra Orr: Do you see any correlation between the work ethic you developed as an agricultural laborer in your teen years and the tireless, prolific energy you bring to writing? Do you think your imagination would have had the same opportunity to flourish if you didn't seek imaginative distraction and escape from your backbreaking work?

Gary Soto: Yes, I do embrace a work ethic. I like getting things done. However, I'm not sure if there is a correlation between the dirty jobs I had as a young man and my work as a writer. I feel in love with poetry writing, but didn't, say, fall in love with chopping beets. Moreover, there are few writers who can sustain, as you say, "backbreaking work" and yet let their creative side blossom. One poet who comes to mind is John Clare, a genius, who worked and wrote brilliantly. But he is an exception. Most writers would prepare to live in poverty rather than to succumb to a nine-to-five job. I mean, I can't imagine Samuel Johnson saying, "Well, I have had enough of these poor shoes, I'm going to go and get a job." He lived for his scholarship, his essays, his dictionary, his country's literary heritage, and his friends. What a great testimony.

Tamra Orr: How much of what you write would you consider autobiographical and how much fictional? Are the stories purely imaginative though set in a world you know and have experienced intimately?

Gary Soto: I have written four autobiographical books—*Living Up the Street*, *Small Faces*, *A Summer Life* and *The Effects of Knut Hamsun*. The rest of the prose that I've done is fiction in that I invent characters and march them through a set of experiences. My adult poetry, as you might guess, is about the self and, thus, is often autobiographical.

Tamra Orr: Can you ever imagine living and writing somewhere other than California? Did you work differently when writing about Japan in *Pacific Crossing*? Did you find the writing process more difficult?

Gary Soto: In an interview the English poet Philip Larkin was asked something like, "Where would you like to travel?" He thought about this for the longest time and responded, "I would like to go to China as long as I can come back on the same day." That's how I feel. I like London and travel there frequently, but I'm not too adventurous in seeing other places. I suppose I'm a bit of a coward this way. I like to wake up in my own bed. I like where I write. I live in Berkeley, California, but have nothing to do with this place. When writing *Pacific Crossing*, I did some research on Japan and then wrote the book because the novel has not so much to do with place as it does with characters.

Tamra Orr: You are one of the most prominent Latino authors to write for children. What other Latino authors do you recommend?

Gary Soto: I envy Victor Martinez's *Parrot in the Oven*. It's a brilliant piece of writing set, by the way, in my hometown of Fresno. It should be read by every twelve year old.

Tamra Orr: You stated in a previous interview that your wife, Carolyn, is the first person to read and review your new work. Is there someone else you depend on for informed and insightful feedback?

Gary Soto: Carolyn, my wife of twenty-nine years, my companion for even longer, has always been my first reader. I'm grateful for her pair of insightful eyes. She makes it so much easier for this writer. I wish I could do her a special favor. She's a clothes designer, and, though it's impossible, I wish I could help her with her last stitches. Of course, my unsteady hands would make a mess of her creations. I would be like a cat in a ball of yarn . . . There are a few others who look at my work, among them Christopher Buckley, the poet and not the essayist, who is like Attila the Hun with his scathing appraisals of my work. He and I have been friends for nearly thirty quick years.

Selected Reviews from *School Library Journal*

Baseball in April and Other Stories
1990
Grades 4–7—Insightful about the characteristics of early adolescents, Soto tells 11 short stories about everyday problems of growing up. Latinos in central California are the focus of the stories, but the events are typical of young teens anywhere in the United States. The main characters try out for Little League teams, take karate lessons, try to get the attention of the opposite sex, and are embarrassed by their grandparents' behavior. These day-to-day events reveal the sensitivity, humor, and vulnerability of today's young

people. The descriptions and dialogue are used to advantage, helping to create and sustain the mood. A glossary of Spanish terms is included. Young readers should easily identify with the situations, emotions, and outcomes presented in these fine short stories.

Crazy Weekend
1993

Grades 4–7—Best friends Hector and Mando, seventh graders from East L.A., spend a weekend with Hector's uncle in Fresno. Uncle Julio, a photographer, takes the boys on an aerial shoot and, by chance, photographs an armored car holdup. After the local paper features the boys in an article concerning the heist, the robbers pledge to teach them a lesson. A couple of brief encounters come to a head when the crooks try to break into Uncle Julio's apartment. This climactic scene is a cross between *Home Alone* and Hitchcock's *Rear Window*, as the two friends continually foil the break-in attempts and eventually subdue and capture the bad guys. Soto's adept character development brings to life the witty, streetwise boys; the bumbling thugs; and the disheveled but well-meaning Julio. Humor is interjected on each page but is seldom forced, and while the ending may be a bit much, it works. As in a number of other books by this talented author, Spanish words and phrases are sprinkled throughout and a glossary is appended. A fast-moving, light read.

Fearless Fernie: Hanging Out with Fernie and Me

2002

Grades 4–6—A collection of 41 short poems by a prolific and gifted writer. The narrator and his friend Fernie are sixth graders with lots on their minds: sports, girls, school, family. Strongly rhythmic, with vivid imagery, the mostly unrhymed selections are universal yet wonderfully particular. Soto smoothly juggles moods, going from funny ("When Fernie was five and school was over for the day, He thought his teacher, Miss Alexander, went into the closet, Stood there among the brooms And maybe a stringy mop") to poignant (in "Guilt," Fernie remembers a friendless classmate in third grade: "Was he still there, in the far corner of the playground? Were the sparrows there, or did they fly elsewhere Once the boy—what's his name—had nothing to give, His lunch all gone, loneliness like crumbs at his feet"). The simple, dynamic sketches sprinkled throughout are just right, providing some humorous and rueful grace notes for this little gem. Overall, this is a wonderful example of distinctive writing with true child appeal. It will make a great classroom read-aloud, and many kids will enjoy it on their own, too.

Jesse

1994

Grades 9 and Up—Set in Fresno, California, in the late 1960s, this coming-of-age tale is told from a Mexican American's point of view. Jesse, 17, is full of self-doubt amid the increasing tensions caused by the war in Vietnam, pressure from within his circle of friends to join the protests of Cesar Chavez, and by the general social and academic milieu of the local community college that he and his older brother attend. The young men share a rundown apartment; they work as day laborers in the fields as well as find and sell junk to earn their way. Already insecure about his lack of experience with girls, Jesse has his nose bloodied by a drunken high-school acquaintance while on his first date. This violence presages other incidents that, although relatively minor, allude to the overarching shadow cast by the war and by the omnipresent draft. The story is poignant, pregnant with unfulfilled promise and dreams of a future that is hoped for but rarely imagined. Simple words reveal universal experiences; innocent and open, Jesse begins to see the real world and discover his place in it. The ending is a bit bleak, suggesting the likelihood of more of the same mindless, backbreaking, spirit-crushing work, with a plethora of unknowns lurking just over the horizon. Readers looking for a finely written, contemplative narrative will appreciate this work.

Local News

1993

Grades 6–12—Much as he did in *Baseball in April* (HBJ, 1990), Soto uses his ability to see the story in everyday experiences and to create ordinary, yet distinctly individual and credible characters to charm readers into another world. He uses his poetic writing style and the Spanish of the Mexican American community in the San Diego area to create 13 new stories for this book. The appended list of terms and phrases will be useful to readers unfamiliar with the language, although many of the terms used are not included in the list. The book will be as popular as a collection of stories about young people as it will be useful for starting discussions regarding sibling rivalry, self-image, growing up, cultures, or writing styles.

Neighborhood Odes

1992

Grades 4 and Up—The rewards of well-chosen words that create vivid, sensitive images await readers of this collection of poems. Through Soto's keen eyes, they see, and will be convinced, that there is poetry in everything. The odes celebrate weddings, the anticipation of fireworks, pets, grandparents, tortillas, and the library. Although Soto is dealing with a Chicano neighborhood, the poetry has a universal appeal. A minor drawback is that the Spanish words are not translated on the page, but in a glossary; to consult it interrupts the reading. Still, children will surely recognize the joy, love, fear, excitement, and adventure Soto brings to life. It is the same sensitivity and clarity found in *Baseball in April* (HBJ, 1990), his collection of short stories. Black-and-white illustrations blend well with the astute verbal imagery. Each selection is an expression of joy and wonder at life's daily pleasures and mysteries.

Petty Crimes

1998

Grades 5 and Up—A colorful potpourri of 10 ironic short stories. Filled with both humor and sadness, these slice-of-life narratives portray both self-reflective and self-involved teen characters who learn valuable life lessons from encounters with family, friends, and antagonists. Mario—a bitter, streetwise teenager—is obsessed with scamming everyone he meets until he gets some of his own medicine thrown back at him. Fourteen-year-old Alma tries to cope with her mother's slow and painful death from cancer by buying back all of the woman's clothes that her grief-stricken father gave to the Salvation Army. Rudy, 17, boxes to prove himself and impress a pretty girl whom he later discovers is the sister of his experienced boxing opponent. Rich in simile and metaphor and sprinkled with Spanish words and phrases that can be understood from context, these simply told memorable stories about Hispanic teens resonate with realism because they deal with concerns most young people have—"Who am I?" and "Am I doing the right thing?"

Selected Reviews from *School Library Journal*

Summer on Wheels

1995

Grades 5-8—Hector and Mando, 13-year-old friends introduced in Crazy Weekend (Scholastic, 1994), return in this story that follows them as they bike from their homes in East Los Angeles to visit Hector's relatives throughout the city. Along the way, Hector earns $100 for appearing in a TV commercial and is rewarded for being the one-millionth attendee at a Dodgers' game. The boys teach bookish cousin Bently how to wrestle, ride a bike, and be more like them; make friends with a spoiled rich girl who challenges them to contests in every sport imaginable, including a paint-ball war; and nearly get mugged until Mando realizes that one of the thugs is his cousin. At their last stop, they get drafted into painting a library mural, which inspires them to paint a rendition of their adventure on Hector's garage. Although the paint-ball episode is a bit overlong, the plot is rollicking, with some dream-come-true aspects, touches of reality, and humor, emphasized by the boys' banter and enhanced by a sprinkling of Spanish words and phrases. Soto's descriptions make the journey vivid and, throughout the boys' scuffles and escapades, they maintain a deep respect for their elders, a love of family, and a healthy curiosity about life. A glossary of Spanish words and phrases is appended, although there is no pronunciation guide.

Taking Sides

1991

Grades 5-7—This light but appealing story deals with cultural differences, moving, and basketball. Eighth-grader Lincoln Mendoza and his mother have just moved from a San Francisco barrio to a wealthy, predominantly white suburb. He misses his Hispanic friends, the noise, camaraderie, and even the dirt and fights in his old neighborhood. Having made first-string on the basketball team, he finds that the coach dislikes him for no good reason. Plot development hinges on an upcoming game between his new school and the old one. As the big day approaches, Lincoln cannot decide which team he wants to win. He's not sure where he truly belongs, but the game helps to clarify this for him. Readers will easily understand the boy's dilemma. The conflicts of old vs. new and Hispanic vs. white culture are clearly delineated. So is the fact that the differences are not as great as they first appear. Lincoln is a typical adolescent:

energetic, likable, moody at times, but adaptable. Other characters are less finely drawn. The coach is the stereotypical obnoxious jock. Lincoln's divorced mother works hard and tries to be a good parent. Her boyfriend Roy is a minor player but he helps Lincoln to deal with his problems. Because of its subject matter and its clear, straightforward prose, the book will be especially good for reluctant readers. A glossary of Spanish words appears at the end of the book.

Timeline

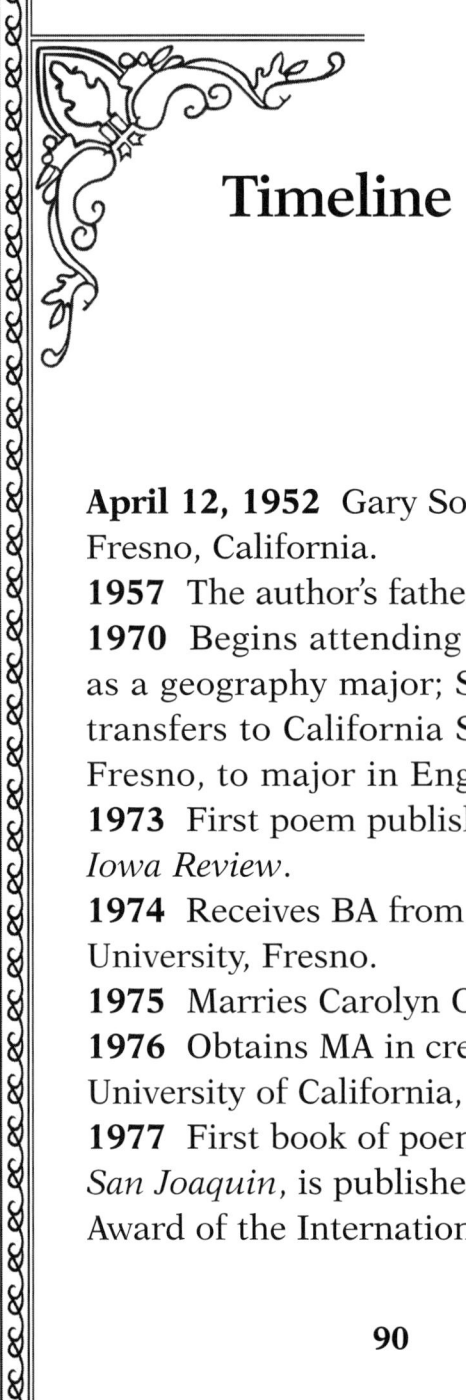

April 12, 1952 Gary Soto is born in Fresno, California.

1957 The author's father, Manuel Soto, dies.

1970 Begins attending Fresno City College as a geography major; Soto eventually transfers to California State University, Fresno, to major in English.

1973 First poem published in the *Iowa Review*.

1974 Receives BA from California State University, Fresno.

1975 Marries Carolyn Oda.

1976 Obtains MA in creative writing from University of California, Irvine.

1977 First book of poems, *The Elements of San Joaquin*, is published. It wins the U.S. Award of the International Poetry Forum.

Timeline

1978 Daughter, Mariko, is born.

1985 Becomes associate professor of English and Chicano studies at the University of California, Berkeley. Soto's book of biographical essays, *Living Up the Street*, wins the American Book Award from the Before Columbus Foundation.

1990 Releases his first two books for young people, *A Fire in My Hands* (poetry) and *Baseball in April and Other Stories* (short stories). *Baseball in April and Other Stories* is named as the American Library Association's Best Book for Young Adults.

1993 Wins the Andrew Carnegie Medal for Excellence in Children's Video for the film *The Pool Party*.

1995 Resigns from his teaching position at the University of California, Berkeley.

1999 Receives the Literature Award from the Hispanic Heritage Foundation, the Author-Illustrator Civil Rights Award from the National Education Association, and the PEN Center West Book Award (for the young adult short story collection *Petty Crimes*).

List of Selected Works

Biographical Essays

Living Up the Street: Narrative Recollections. San Francisco, CA: Strawberry Hill Press, 1985.

California Childhood: Recollections and Stories of the Golden State. Berkeley, CA: Creative Arts Books, 1988.

Lesser Evils: Ten Quartets. Houston, TX: Arte Publico Press, 1988.

A Summer Life. Lebanon, NH: University Press of New England, 1990.

The Effects of Knut Hamsun on a Fresno Boy: Recollections and Short Essays. New York: Persea Books, 2000.

List of Selected Works

Biographies

Jessie de la Cruz: Profile of a United Farm Worker. New York: Persea Books, 2000.

Cesar Chavez: A Hero for Everyone. New York: Simon and Schuster, 2003.

Children's Books

The Cat's Meow. San Francisco, CA: Strawberry Hill Press, 1987.

The Pool Party. New York: Delacorte Press, 1993.

Too Many Tamales. New York: Putnam, 1993.

The Skirt. New York: Yearling, 1994.

Boys at Work. New York: Delacorte Press, 1995.

Chato's Kitchen. New York: Putnam, 1995.

The Old Man and His Door. New York: Putnam, 1996.

Snapshots from the Wedding. New York: Putnam, 1997.

Big Bushy Mustache. New York: Knopf, 1998.

Chato and the Party Animals. New York: Putnam, 2000.

My Little Car. New York: Putnam, 2000.

If the Shoe Fits. New York: Putnam, 2002.

Novio Boy: A Play. New York: Harcourt Brace, 1997.

Nerdlandia: A Play. New York: Putnam, 1999.

Young Adult Poetry

A Fire in My Hands: A Book of Poems. New York: Scholastic, 1990.

Neighborhood Odes. San Diego, CA: Harcourt Brace, 1992.

Canto Familiar. New York: Harcourt Brace, 1995.

Fearless Fernie: Hanging Out with Fernie and Me. New York: G. P. Putnam's Sons, 2002.

Adult Poetry

The Elements of San Joaquin. Pittsburgh, PA: University of Pittsburgh Press, 1977.

The Tale of Sunlight. Pittsburgh, PA: University of Pittsburgh Press, 1978.

Where Sparrows Work Hard. Pittsburgh, PA: University of Pittsburgh Press, 1981.

Black Hair. Pittsburgh, PA: University of Pittsburgh Press, 1985.

Who Will Know Us? San Francisco, CA: Chronicle Books, 1990.

Home Course in Religion. San Francisco, CA: Chronicle Books, 1991.

New and Selected Poems. San Francisco, CA: Chronicle Books, 1995.

Junior College. San Francisco, CA: Chronicle Books, 1997.

A Natural Man. San Francisco, CA: Chronicle Books, 1999.
One Kind of Faith. San Francisco, CA: Chronicle Books, 2003.

Young Adult Novels
Taking Sides. San Diego, CA: Harcourt Brace, 1991.
Pacific Crossing. New York: Harcourt Brace, 1992.
Crazy Weekend. New York: Scholastic, 1994.
Jesse. New York: Harcourt Brace, 1994.
Summer on Wheels. New York: Scholastic, 1995.
Buried Onions. New York: Harcourt Brace, 1997.
The Afterlife. New York: Harcourt Children's Books, 2003.

Young Adult Short Story Collections
Baseball in April and Other Stories. San Diego: Harcourt Brace, 1990.
Local News. New York: Harcourt Brace, 1993.
Petty Crimes. New York: Harcourt Brace, 1998.

List of Selected Awards

"Discovery" *The Nation,* The Joan Leiman Jacobson Poetry Prize (1975)
The Bess Hokin Prize and the Levinson Award from the literary magazine *Poetry* (1978)
Guggenheim Fellowship (1979)
The Author-Illustrator Civil Rights Award from the National Education Association (1999)
The Literature Award from the Hispanic Heritage Foundation (1999)
National Endowment for the Arts Fellowships for Creative Writing (twice)

The Elements of San Joaquin (1977)
Academy of American Poets Prize (1975)
The U.S. Award of the International Poetry Forum (1976)

List of Selected Awards

Living Up the Street (1985)
Before Columbus Foundation American Book Award (1985)

Baseball in April and Other Stories (1990)
The American Library Association's Best Book for Young Adults (1990)
The California Library Association's John and Patricia Beatty Award (1991)

The Pool Party (1992; video)
Andrew Carnegie Medal for Excellence in Children's Video (1993)

Too Many Tamales (1993)
Book for Youth Editors' Choices, *Booklist* (1993)

New and Selected Poems (1995)
Finalist for the *Los Angeles Times* Book Award and the National Book Award (1995)

Summer on Wheels (1995)
The California Library Association's John and Patricia Beatty Award (1996)

Petty Crimes (1998)
The PEN Center West Book Award (1999)

Glossary

autobiographical Relating to one's own life.
barrio Spanish-speaking neighborhood in the United States, especially in the Southwest.
biography A history, usually written, of a person's life.
Chicano An American of Mexican descent.
episodic Made up of a series of separate scenes or stories.
ethnicity Belonging to a particular cultural, racial, national, tribal, or religious group.
heritage Tradition.
illiterate Unable to read or write.
incessant Unending, continuous.

Glossary

inevitable Unavoidable.
libretto The text of a dramatic musical work, such as an opera.
monotonous Dull, unchanging, or uniform.
nostalgic Recalling with fondness things or people from the past.
prose A form of literary writing that is different from poetry in that its rhythms and patterns more resemble everyday speech.
reliance Dependence.
tedious Tiresome, dull, boring.

For More Information

Web Sites

Due to the changing nature of Internet links, the Rosen Publishing Group, Inc., has developed an online list of Web sites related to the subject of this book. This site is updated regularly. Please use this link to access the list:

http://www.rosenlinks.com/lab/gaso

For Further Reading

Catalano, Julie. *The Mexican Americans*. Broomall, PA: Chelsea House Publishers, 1995.

Lee, Don. "About Gary Soto." *Ploughshares* 21.1 (Spring 1995).

Macmillan Profiles: Latino Americans. New York: Macmillan Library Reference, 1999.

Martinez, Victor. *Parrot in the Oven: Mi Vida*. New York: Rayo, 1998.

Morey, Janet, and Wendy Dunn. *Famous Mexican Americans*. New York: Puffin, 1997.

Murphy, Patricia. "Inventing Lunacy: An Interview with Gary Soto." *Hayden's Ferry* Review 18 (Spring-Summer 1996).

Nava, Yolanda, ed. *It's All in the Frijoles: 100 Famous Latinos Share Real-Life Stories, Time-Tested Dichos, Favorite Folktales, and Inspiring Words of Wisdom.* New York: Fireside, 2000.

Perl, Lila. *North Across the Border: The Story of the Mexican Americans.* Salt Lake City, UT: Benchmark Books, 2002.

Soto, Gary, ed. *Pieces of the Heart: New Chicano Fiction.* San Francisco, CA: Chronicle Books, 1993.

Bibliography

"Gary Soto's Biography." Scholastic.com (division of Scholastic, Inc.). 2000. Retrieved May 2004 (http://www2.scholastic.com/teachers/authorsandbooks/authorstudies/authorhome.jhtml;schsessionid=4PBHE23QBZTU0CQVAKUCFFIKCUBJYIV4?authorID=89&collateralID=5363&displayName=Interview+Transcript).

"Gary Soto." Videocassette. Santa Fe, NM: Lannan Foundation, 1995.

Lee, Don. "About Gary Soto." *Ploughshares* 21.1 (Spring 1995): 188–192.

Macmillan Profiles: Latino Americans. New York: Macmillan Library Reference, 1999.

Norton Anthology of Modern Poetry. 2d ed. New York: W. W. Norton, 1978.

Silvey, Anita. *Help Wanted: Short Stories about Young People Working*. Toronto, Ontario: Little Brown and Company, 1997.

Soto, Gary. *Afterlife*. New York: Harcourt Children's Books, 2003.

Soto, Gary. *Canto Familiar*. New York: Harcourt Brace, 1995.

Soto, Gary. T*he Effects of Knut Hamsun on a Fresno Boy: Recollections and Short Essays*. New York: Persea Books, 2000.

Soto, Gary. *Fearless Fernie: Hanging Out with Fernie and Me*. New York: Putnam, 2002.

Soto, Gary. "Frequently Asked Questions." The Official Gary Soto Web Site. Retrieved May 2004 (http://www.garysoto.com/faq.html).

Soto, Gary. *Lesser Evils: Ten Quartets*. Houston, TX: Arte Publico Press, 1988.

Soto, Gary. *Living Up the Street: Narrative Recollections*. San Francisco, CA: Strawberry Hill Press, 1985.

Soto, Gary. "A Red Palm." PoemHunter.com. Retrieved May 2004 (http://www.poemhunter.com/p/m/poem.asp?poet=10856&poem=175975).

Soto, Gary. *Small Faces*. Houston, TX: Arte Publico Press, 1986.

Soto, Gary. *A Summer Life*. New York: Laurel Leaf, 1991.

Bibliography

Strunk, Sherry. "Gary Soto." University of Nebraska, Omaha. Retrieved May 2004 (http://www.unomaha.edu/!unochlit/soto.html).

Wilson, Etta. "Gary Soto—A Mexican-American Voice that Speaks for All." Book Page. 1998. Retrieved May 2004 (http://www.bookpage.com/9805bp/gary_soto.html).

Source Notes

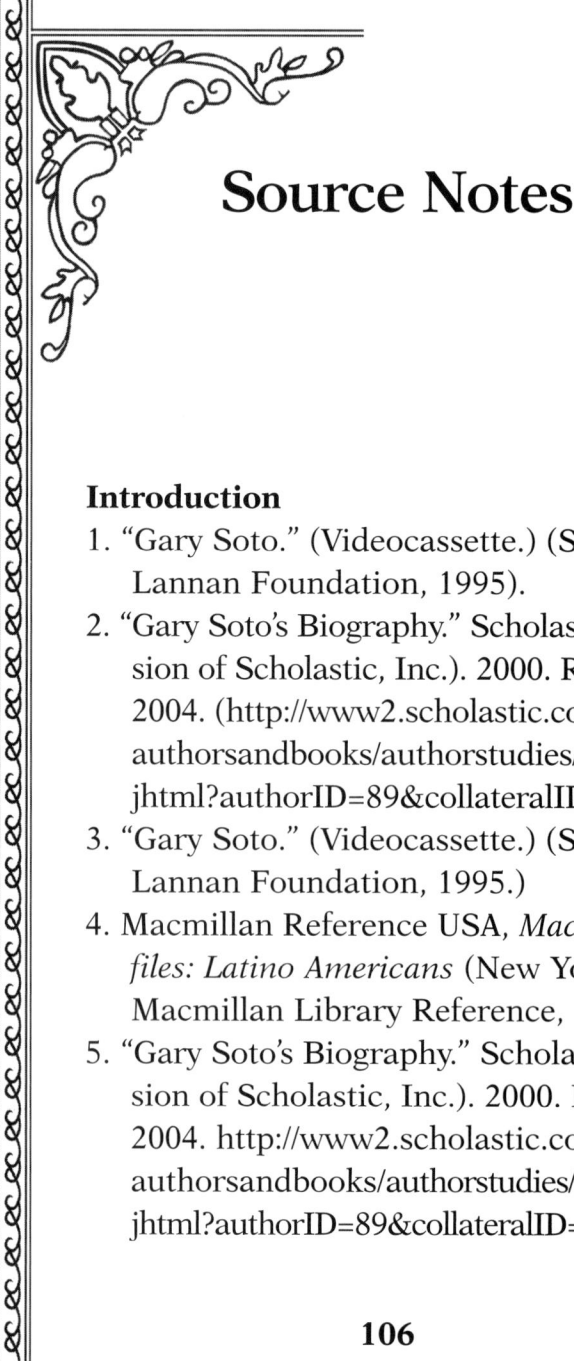

Introduction
1. "Gary Soto." (Videocassette.) (Santa Fe, NM: Lannan Foundation, 1995).
2. "Gary Soto's Biography." Scholastic.com (division of Scholastic, Inc.). 2000. Retrieved May 2004. (http://www2.scholastic.com/teachers/authorsandbooks/authorstudies/authorhome.jhtml?authorID=89&collateralID=5285).
3. "Gary Soto." (Videocassette.) (Santa Fe, NM: Lannan Foundation, 1995.)
4. Macmillan Reference USA, *Macmillan Profiles: Latino Americans* (New York: Macmillan Library Reference, 1999), p. 349.
5. "Gary Soto's Biography." Scholastic.com (division of Scholastic, Inc.). 2000. Retrieved May 2004. http://www2.scholastic.com/teachers/authorsandbooks/authorstudies/authorhome.jhtml?authorID=89&collateralID=5285

Source Notes

6. Macmillan Reference USA, *Macmillan Profiles: Latino Americans* (New York: Macmillan Library Reference, 1999), p. 349.

Chapter 1
1. Gary Soto, "A Red Palm," PoemHunter.com. Retrieved May 2004 (http://www.poemhunter.com/p/m/poem.asp?poet=10856&poem=175975)
2. Gary Soto, "This Man," *The Effects of Knut Hamsun on a Fresno Boy: Recollections and Short Essays* (New York: Persea Books, 2000), p. 68.
3. Don Lee, "About Gary Soto," *Ploughshares*, Volume 21, Number 1, Spring 1995, pp. 188–192.
4. Gary Soto, "The Jacket," *The Effects of Knut Hamsun on a Fresno Boy: Recollections and Short Essays* (New York: Persea Books, 2000), p. 8.
5. Gary Soto, "One Last Time," *Living Up the Street: Narrative Recollections* (San Francisco: Strawberry Hill Press, 1985), p. 107.
6. Gary Soto, "Blue," *Small Faces* (Houston, TX: Arte Publico Press, 1986), p. 88.

Chapter 2
1. Don Lee, "About Gary Soto," *Ploughshares*, Volume 21, Number 1, Spring 1995, pp. 188–192.
2. Ibid.
3. Gary Soto. "Frequently Asked Questions." The Official Gary Soto Web Site. Retrieved May 2004. (http://www.garysoto.com/faq.html).

4. Gary Soto, "Getting It Done," *The Effects of Knut Hamsun on a Fresno Boy: Recollections and Short Essays* (New York: Persea Books, 2000), pp. 186–187.

Chapter 3

1. Joel Shoemaker, *School Library Journal* review of *Jesse*, 1994.
2. Gary Soto, "Getting It Done," *The Effects of Knut Hamsun on a Fresno Boy: Recollections and Short Essays* (New York: Persea Books, 2000), p. 185.
3. Gary Soto, *Buried Onions* (New York: Harcourt Children's Books, 1997).
4. Ibid.
5. Gary Soto, *Afterlife* (New York: Harcourt Children's Books, 2003), p. 4.

Chapter 4

1. Ann Welton, *School Library Journal* review of *Chato and the Party Animals*, 2000.
2. Ann Welton, *School Library Journal* review of *The Skirt*, 1992.

Chapter 5

1. Gary Soto, "Wind (2)," *Norton Anthology of Modern Poetry*, Second ed. (New York: W. W. Norton, 1978).
2. Gary Soto, "Rain," *Norton Anthology of Modern Poetry*. Second ed. (New York: W. W. Norton, 1978).

Source Notes

3. Gary Soto, "Drought," *Norton Anthology of Modern Poetry*. Second ed. (New York: W. W. Norton, 1978).
4. Ibid.
5. "Gary Soto." (Videocassette.) (Santa Fe, NM: Lannan Foundation, 1995).
6. Gary Soto, "Papi's Menudo," *Canto Familiar* (New York: Harcourt Brace, 1995), pp. 1–3.
7. Gary Soto, "Fall Football," *Fearless Fernie: Hanging Out with Fernie and Me* (New York: Putnam, 2002), p. 18.
8. Gary Soto, "Guilt," *Fearless Fernie: Hanging Out with Fernie and Me* (New York: Putnam, 2002), p. 13.
9. Gary Soto, "On the Escalator at Macy's," *Fearless Fernie: Hanging Out with Fernie and Me* (New York: Putnam, 2002), p. 40.
10. Ibid.
11. Mary T. Garrity, *School Library Journal* review of *Gary Soto: New and Selected Poems*, 1995.

Chapter 6

1. Gary Soto. "Frequently Asked Questions," The Official Gary Soto Web Site. Retrieved May 2004 (http://www.garysoto.com/faq.html).
2. "Gary Soto's Biography." Scholastic.com (division of Scholastic, Inc.). 2000. Retrieved May 2004. http://www2.scholastic.com/teachers/authorsandbooks/authorstudies/authorhome.jhtml?authorID=89&collateralID=5285

Index

A
Afterlife, The, 38–39
Amnesia in a Republican County, 38
"Animals All Around" (essay), 19

B
Baseball in April and Other Stories, 29, 31
Big Bushy Mustache, 43–44
Bike, The, 9
"Blue" (essay), 17–18
Buried Onions, 36–37

C
Canto Familiar, 53, 57
Chato and the Party Animals, 42–43
Chato's Day of Dead, 43
Chato Goes Cruisin', 43
Chato's Kitchen, 42

Chavez, Cesar, 69
Crazy Weekend, 33–34

D
de la Cruz, Jessie, 68–69
"Drought" (poem), 52–53

E
Effects of Knut Hamsun on a Fresno Boy, The, 14
  excerpt from, 25
Elements of San Joaquin, The, 24

F
Fearless Fernie: Hanging Out with Fernie and Me, 59–66
Fire in My Hands, A, 29
Fresno School of Poets, 23

G
"Getting It Done" (essay), 35

110

Index

I
If the Shoe Fits, 45–46

J
"Jacket, The" (essay), 16–17
Jesse, 33

L
Living Up the Street, 26
Local News, 31

M
Mexican Revolution, 12
Morales, Alejandro, 8
"Music for Fun and Profit" (poem), 57–59

N
Neighborhood Odes, 30–31
Nerdlandia (play), 9, 67–68
Nickel and Dime, 38
"No-Guitar Blues, The" (story), 35–36
Norton Anthology of Modern Poetry, 50–53
Novio Boy (play), 9, 67

O
Oda, Carolyn (wife), 23–24, 70
Old Man and His Door, The, 46–47
"One Last Time" (essay), 15, 17

P
Pacific Crossing, 32
"Papi's Menudo" (poem), 53–57
Petty Crimes, 37

Poetry Lover, 38
Pool Party, The, 9, 33

R
"Rain" (poem), 51–52

S
Skirt, The, 44–45
Small Faces, 19, 26
Snapshots from a Wedding, 47
Soto, Gary
  adult fiction, 8, 9, 28, 38, 41
  awards, 25, 26, 29, 33, 37, 42
  biographies, 68–70
  childhood, 11–20, 28
  daughter, 24–25, 70
  education, 21–23
  essays, 9, 10, 14, 15, 16–18, 24, 26, 28, 35
  family, 11–14, 15, 64–65
  films, 9, 33
  hobbies, 70–71
  literary influences, 22, 49
  marriage, 22
  Mexican heritage, 7–8, 11–12, 15, 28, 29, 41–42, 69, 72
  picture books, 8, 9, 28, 40, 41, 42–43, 44, 45, 57, 67, 71
  poetry, 8–9, 10, 13, 22–23, 24, 25–26, 35, 48, 49–66, 71
  poetry collections, 24, 26, 29, 30
  themes in writing, 8, 28, 29, 31–32, 38, 39–40, 47, 48, 50
  at University of California,

111

Berkeley, 27, 34–35
on writing, 9–10
young adult fiction, 29, 33, 36, 38, 41
Soto, Manuel (father), 12, 13–14
Soto, Mariko (daughter), 24–25, 70
Summer Life, A, 29, 30
Summer on Wheels, 34

T
Taking Sides, 29–30
Too Many Tamales, 44

V
Vietnam War, 20, 21, 33

W
"Wind (2)" (poem), 50–51

About the Author

Tamra Orr is the author of more than forty nonfiction books for kids and families. She lives in Portland, Oregon, with her husband and four children, ages eight to twenty. She spends much of her time reading and says little in life is as exciting as finding a great new author.

Photo Credits

Cover, p. 2 courtesy of Gary Soto.

Series Design: Tahara Anderson; **Editor:** John Kemmerer